Use Your Eye, Let's Classify!

Kelly Doudna

Consulting Editors, Diane Craig, M.A./Reading Specialist
and Susan Kosel, M.A. Education

Published by ABDO Publishing Company, 4940 Viking Drive, Edina, Minnesota 55435.

Credits
Edited by: Pam Price
Curriculum Coordinator: Nancy Tuminelly
Cover and Interior Design and Production: Mighty Media
Photo Credits: AbleStock, Comstock, iStockphoto/Nancy Louie, Photodisc, Wewerka Photography

Library of Congress Cataloging-in-Publication Data

Doudna, Kelly, 1963-
    Use your eye, let's classify! / Kelly Doudna.
     p. cm. -- (Science made simple)
    ISBN 10 1-59928-620-3 (hardcover)
    ISBN 10 1-59928-621-1 (paperback)

    ISBN 13 978-1-59928-620-4 (hardcover)
    ISBN 13 978-1-59928-621-1 (paperback)
    1. Set theory--Juvenile literature. 2. Similarity judgment--Juvenile literature. I. Title. II. Series: Science made simple (ABDO Publishing Company)

    QA248.D68 2007
    511.3'22--dc22

                                                                2006012563

SandCastle Level: Transitional

SandCastle™ books are created by a professional team of educators, reading specialists, and content developers around five essential components—phonemic awareness, phonics, vocabulary, text comprehension, and fluency—to assist young readers as they develop reading skills and strategies and increase their general knowledge. All books are written, reviewed, and leveled for guided reading, early reading intervention, and Accelerated Reader® programs for use in shared, guided, and independent reading and writing activities to support a balanced approach to literacy instruction. The SandCastle™ series has four levels that correspond to early literacy development. The levels help teachers and parents select appropriate books for young readers.

Emerging Readers	**Beginning Readers**	**Transitional Readers**	**Fluent Readers**
(no flags)	(1 flag)	(2 flags)	(3 flags)

These levels are meant only as a guide. All levels are subject to change.

To **classify** is to group items that have something in common. Shape, color, material, and use are different ways you can classify. There is often more than one way to classify something.

Words used to classify:

alike	resemble
also	same
both	similar
like	sort
looks like	

A 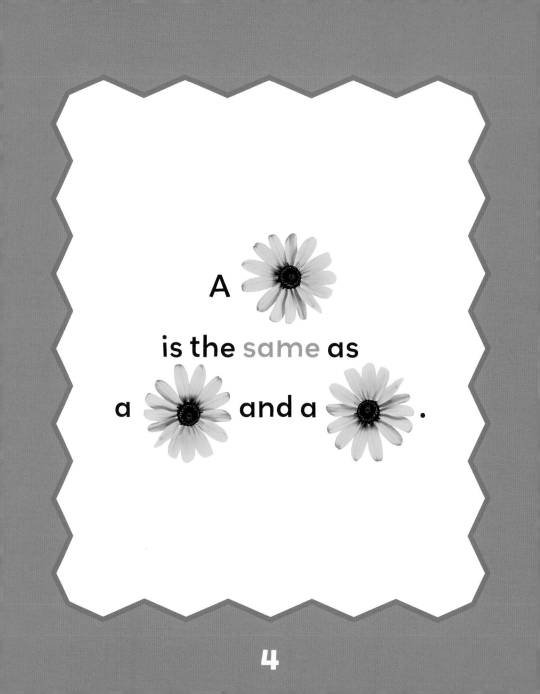 is the same as

a and a .

A  is similar to a .

A  is like a .

A  and a

are both balls.

A

is also a ball.

A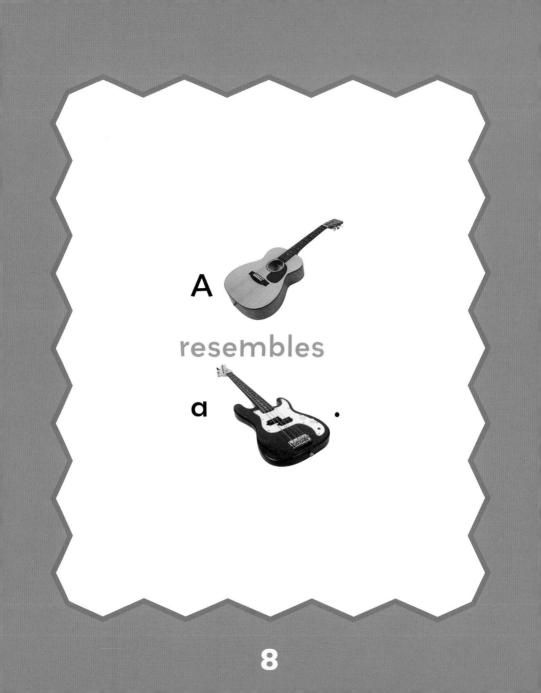

resembles

a .

A

looks like

a .

Use Your Eye, Let's Classify!

Here's a guy
who can classify.
Let's watch how Reggie
sorts fruits and veggies.

Some are roots,
and others are
fruits!

Reggie knows it's okay
to group another way.
He doesn't find it bizarre
to sort by the shape
things are.

It's not wrong
to say
they're long!

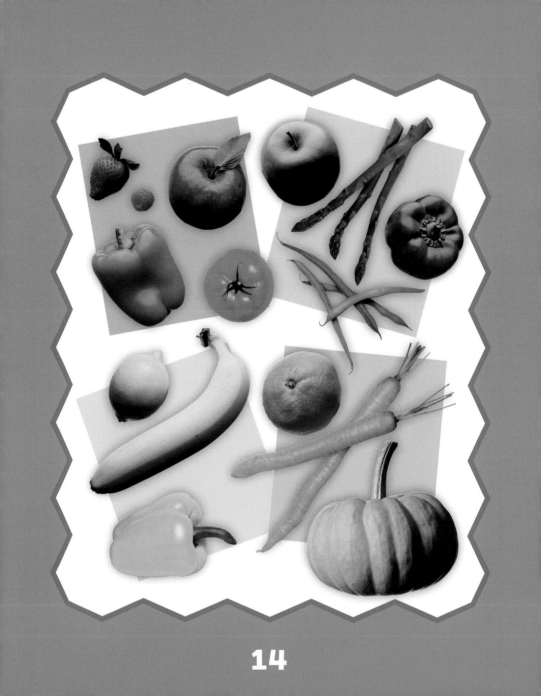

14

Reggie can sort the food instead by whether it's green, orange, yellow, or red. You can apply what you know when you classify!

I will take an orange and pair it with a lovely carrot!

15

I Can Classify Every Day!

Many kinds of animals live at the zoo. I can classify animals as mammals, reptiles, amphibians, birds, or fish.

The zoo is a fun place to learn about classifying!

I can sort vehicles into cars, trucks, buses, airplanes, trains, and boats.

There are many kinds of vehicles.

Items in the grocery store are grouped so that items that are alike are together.

Beef and chicken are both in the meat department. Milk and cheese are both in the dairy department.

I can even classify at school! First graders go to one class together. Second graders go to another class together.

What other ways can you think of to classify?

Glossary

classify – to put things in groups according to their characteristics.

group – to put items together.

resemble – to be alike or similar to.

similar – having characteristics in common.

sort – to group according to characteristics such as size, color, or shape.